Oril and the mon hated balloons

by John Agard
Illustrated by Jenny Stowe

There was this monster who hated balloons.
He was a very weepy-eyed monster with droopy-yellow eyes going down to his cheeks, and he had a forever thinking kind of face.

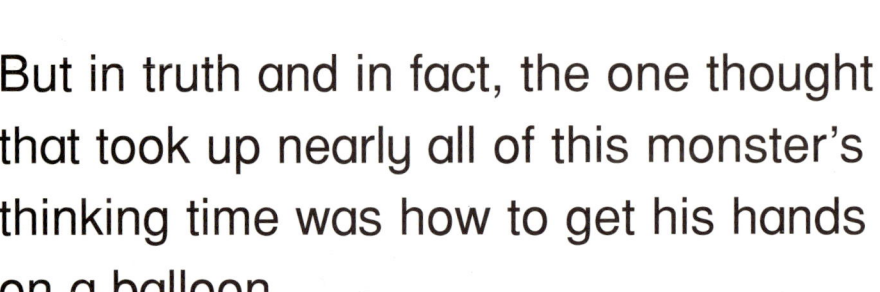

But in truth and in fact, the one thought that took up nearly all of this monster's thinking time was how to get his hands on a balloon.
Yes, the sound of a balloon going pop was a high moment in this monster's life. That was the closest he ever came to a smile.

You see, sadness was this monster's only friend, and because balloons always looked so happy he really hated them.

To him, they were big silly blobs and he could not understand why people would want to blow them up.

This monster decided that the only reason was because people could not keep their happiness inside.
No, they had to show off their happiness.

The slightest excuse and they're hanging balloons again, or blobs, as the monster called them.

So be so, this monster thought to himself,
(for this was his favourite expression
whenever he decided to do something).
So be so. Let them hang the blobs.
I'll lay them low.
Pop every last one.

Moonlight was his favourite time for balloon-popping, but one bright summer day, Weepy-Eye was walking through the streets when he spotted a big fat balloon coming towards him on a piece of string before it made one turn in the breeze and got hooked onto a tree.

Weepy-Eye, who was taller than your mum, your dad, or your teacher, reached out to take the balloon down from the tree for Weepy-Eye was no fool.
He was thinking that maybe other balloons were following this one, so fat and yellow like a sister to the moon.
He stared at the balloon with a faraway look. All the while Weepy-Eye was thinking, so be so, wait and see, then lay low the blob.

Just then a little voice said,
"Can I have back my balloon please?"
It was a little girl half-squeezing her body
through the garden fence of a house
where a birthday party was going on and
music coming from a tape-recorder on the
grass and children running around
screaming.

Right there on the grass was a table laid out with a birthday cake and cheese sandwiches and bread fruit fritters and shining sweets and paper cups with bright drink. But it wasn't these snacks and nibbles that excited Weepy-Eye at all.

His droopy-yellow eyes were just goggling at the sight of all those balloons lying around on the grass, some like wriggly pink snakes,

for when the children got bored they just dropped their balloons on the grass and went back to the table for another handful of cake, or carried on chasing one another.

Our friend, Weepy-Eye, was wishing
he could join them, so when the little girl,
whose name was Oriki, said
"Thank you for getting back my balloon,"
and "Would you like to come to my party?"
Weepy-Eye felt this was his chance.

"I got six candles on my cake today,"
Oriki told her new-found friend.
"And I blew them all out.
I was supposed to make a wish,
and I made six, and I said the words
like a poem inside myself."

And Weepy-Eye couldn't stop himself stamping on one of the wriggly balloons on the grass until the snakey thing popped out its breath.

Then he picked up a big red balloon and began to bite into it like some enormous melon, which the children thought was very funny, especially when the balloon made one loud pop.

"That's the man who saved my balloon from the tree," Oriki was telling her mum, who was just saying to Oriki's dad that they must think of something else to entertain the children. They were tired of playing "There's a Brown Girl in the Ring Tra-la-la-la-la."

They must have played that record at least a dozen times, dancing round in a ring till she felt her poor head was beginning to feel like a dizzy sugar-in-a-plum. Then, as if in answer to her prayers, there were the children gathered round this droopy-eye stranger, bombarding him with balloon after balloon, and he was busy popping like nobody's business.

Although she didn't know where he had appeared from, Oriki's mum felt he looked harmless, and at least he was stopping the children from getting bored.
In fact, she was pleased to hear Oriki, the birthday girl, making up a little rhyme of her own, and all the other children joining in.

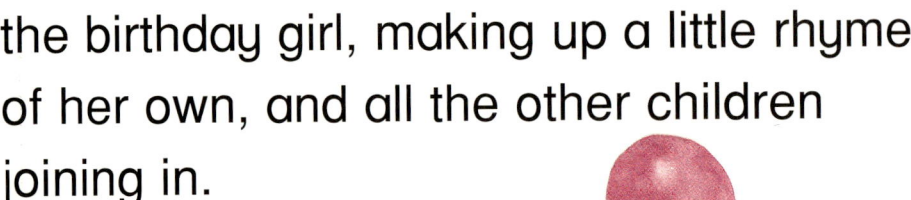

Balloon number one
Balloon number two
Pop the red
Pop the blue
Pop one for me
Pop one for you

And while the children were jumping and screaming, Weepy-Eye was showered with balloons of all colours like enormous bubbles, and the monster was having the popping spree of his life.

The truth is he got the children so excited, and they were screaming so much, Oriki's mum was beginning to wonder how she'd be able to quiet them down.
She might have to end up telling them one of those stories her own mother used to tell her on moonlit nights back in the Caribbean.

But with just one balloon left to burst, Weepy-Eye was now drifting into a faraway broody mood, and that last balloon was the very same one he had saved from the tree for Oriki. Something was stopping Weepy-Eye from popping that one big yellow balloon, and he kept staring into it as if he was staring into the moon itself.

"You can keep it, Mister Balloon-Face," Oriki said.
No one had ever called him by that name before, and the circle of children around him echoed the name Oriki had made up: "Yes, keep it, Mister Balloon-Face, keep it Mister Balloon-Face."

Weepy-Eye flickered his droopy-yellow eyes like two small saucers of light, and as he waved goodbye to the children, he disappeared down the street still holding Oriki's yellow balloon by the end of the string and wishing for the first time in his life that a balloon would never pop.